Mars

ELAINE LANDAU

Children's Press®
An Imprint of Scholastic Inc.
New York   Toronto   London   Auckland   Sydney
Mexico City   New Delhi   Hong Kong
Danbury, Connecticut

Content Consultant

Michelle Yehling

Astronomy Education Consultant

Aurora, Illinois

Reading Consultant

Linda Cornwell

Literacy Consultant

Carmel, Indiana

Library of Congress Cataloging-in-Publication Data

Landau, Elaine.
 Mars / by Elaine Landau.
    p. cm. — (A true book)
 Includes bibliographical references and index.
 ISBN-13: 978-0-531-12560-1 (lib. bdg.)   978-0-531-14790-0 (pbk.)
 ISBN-10: 0-531-12560-2 (lib. bdg.)   0-531-14790-8 (pbk.)
 1. Mars (Planet)—Juvenile literature. I. Title. II. Series.
 QB641.L364 2008
 523.43—dc22   2007012260

All rights reserved. Published in 2008 by Children's Press, an imprint of Scholastic Inc.
Published simultaneously in Canada. Printed in China. 62
SCHOLASTIC, CHILDREN'S PRESS, A TRUE BOOK, and associated logos are trademarks
and/or registered trademarks of Scholastic Inc.
1 2 3 4 5 6 7 8 9 10 R 17 16 15 14 13 12 11 10 09 08

Find the Truth!

Everything you are about to read is true *except* for one of the sentences on this page.

Which one is **TRUE**?

T or F   You would weigh more on Mars than you do on Earth.

T or F   There is a crater on Mars that looks like a happy face.

Find the answer in this book.

Contents

THE **BIG** TRUTH!

Put on a Happy Face

About every two years, the sun, Earth, and Mars line up with one another.

4 The Moons of Mars

5 Missions to Mars

Mars's surface is very similar to Earth's. Mars's mountains and volcanoes were formed in the same way that Earth's are.

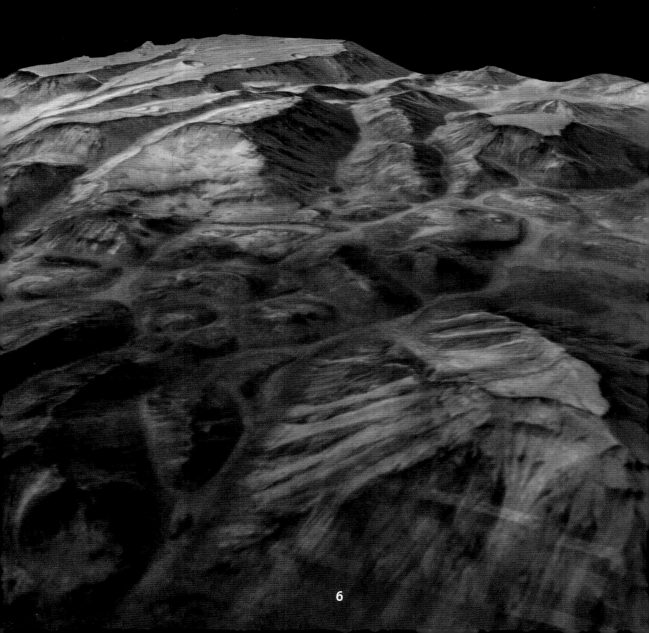

CHAPTER 1

A Trip to Mars

Mars and Venus are Earth's next-door neighbors in the solar system.

Have you ever wondered if there is life on other planets? People have wondered the same thing for centuries. They have often looked to Mars for clues. Let's take a trip to Mars to find out why.

Earth and Venus are close in size.

Many **astronomers** think there might once have been life on Mars. There may be *human* life there someday. Because Mars is closer to Earth than most other planets, it might be possible for humans to travel there.

The distance between Mars and Earth varies from about 35 million miles (56 million kilometers) to more than 249 million miles (401 million km).

It would take about eight months to travel to Mars in a spaceship.

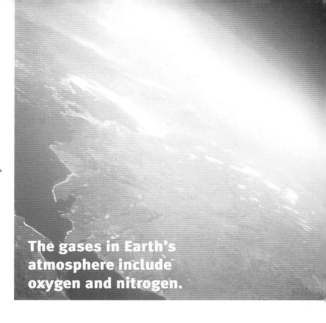

The gases in Earth's atmosphere include oxygen and nitrogen.

Your trip would begin when you blasted off in a spaceship. Soon you would pass through the Earth's **atmosphere**. An atmosphere is the blanket of gases that surrounds a planet or a moon. Next, you would enter outer space.

Your trip through space would look like one very long night. You would be surrounded by darkness all the time. Without Earth's atmosphere in the way though, you would be able to see thousands of bright stars.

Though Mars is closer to Earth than Jupiter is, Mars is dimmer in the night sky.

From far away, Mars looks like a star with a red-orange glow. That's why some people call it the "red planet." As you got closer, however, you would see color that looks like butterscotch, caramel, and rust mixed together. Mars has gray areas, as well.

As you flew even closer to Mars, you might notice the mountains, valleys, and volcanoes on the planet's surface. Mars is a solid planet, so your spaceship could find a place to land. It would not be an easy place to go sightseeing, though. It is extremely cold on Mars. There isn't enough air to breathe. You would have to put on a space suit before you could go exploring.

Using information collected by spacecraft, astronomers created this image of a deep valley on Mars.

Mars has many different types of rocks. Many of them were formed from lava.

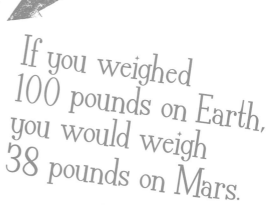

If you weighed 100 pounds on Earth, you would weigh 38 pounds on Mars.

You would feel very light as you hiked across Mars. If you jumped up into the air, you would jump higher than you would on Earth. That's because **gravity** on Mars is weaker than gravity on Earth. Gravity is the force that pulls you down toward the center of a planet.

Why does Mars have less gravity? What makes the planet so cold? What gives it its color? Why do scientists believe that life may have existed there? Let's find out more about Mars.

Martian Canals?

If you look at Mars through a telescope, you might see lines running across the planet. Around 1895, an American astronomer named Percival Lowell decided that the lines were canals. Canals are like rivers, except they are man-made—or *Martian-*made, in this case. Lowell thought that Martians had dug these canals.

Lowell wrote three books about life on Mars. Many people thought Lowell was right. Much later, photos from spacecraft proved him wrong. The photos showed no canals and no Martians that might have dug them. From far away, Mars's natural features just looked like lines, but they really weren't.

This drawing from 1877 maps the markings that some people thought were canals on Mars's surface.

In this image, the lines that go through the planets show the paths the planets take around the sun. The lines around the planets show the paths of their moons.

moon

sun

Earth

Mars

14

CHAPTER 2

Mars in the Solar System

Some of Mars's color might come from rusty rocks!

Mars is one of eight planets in our **solar system**. A solar system is like a giant neighborhood. The other planets are Mercury, Venus, Earth, Jupiter, Saturn, Uranus, and Neptune. All of these planets circle around the sun. The solar system also has at least 162 moons, many icy **comets**, and rocky **asteroids**.

Mars's Solar System

Pluto (dwarf planet)

Uranus

Mars

Jupiter

Mercury

Mars

- Fourth planet from the sun
- Seventh-largest planet
- Diameter: 4,222 mi. (6,794 km)
- One day equals 24 hours, 37 minutes
- One year equals 687 Earth days

16

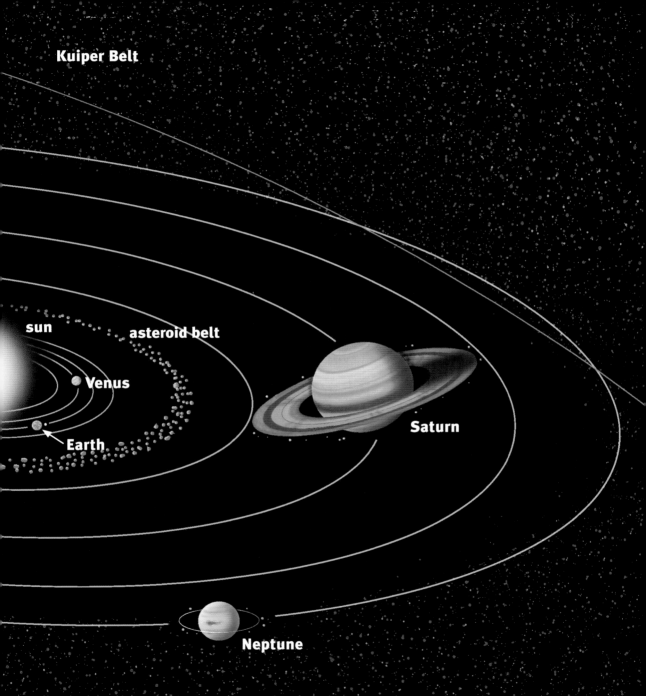

Kuiper Belt

sun

asteroid belt

Venus

Earth

Saturn

Neptune

Mars on the Move

Like the other planets in our solar system, Mars **orbits**, or travels around, the sun. It travels in a flattened circular path called an ellipse (ee-LIPS).

Earth is the third planet from the sun, and Mars is the fourth. Because Mars is farther away from the sun than Earth, it travels around the sun in a larger ellipse.

A year is equal to the time it takes for a planet to orbit the sun once. Earth orbits the sun in about 365 days. Mars orbits the sun in 687 Earth days. This means that a year on Mars is almost twice as long as a year on Earth.

If you are 10 years old on Earth, you would be only five years old in Mars years.

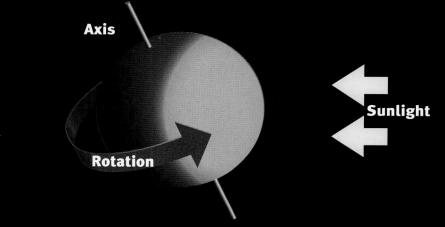

Axis

Sunlight

Rotation

The red arrow in this diagram shows the direction of Mars's rotation. It is daytime on the side that faces the sun. As the planet rotates, new parts move into the sunlight.

While Mars orbits the sun, it also spins on its **axis**. An axis is an imaginary line that runs from north to south through the center of a planet. The time it takes a planet to spin around once on its axis equals one day. One day on Earth is 23 hours, 56 minutes long. One day on Mars is 24 hours, 37 minutes long. So a day on Mars is just 41 minutes longer than a day on Earth.

Like Earth, Mars has north and south poles. The whitish area in this image shows the ice cap at one of Mars's poles.

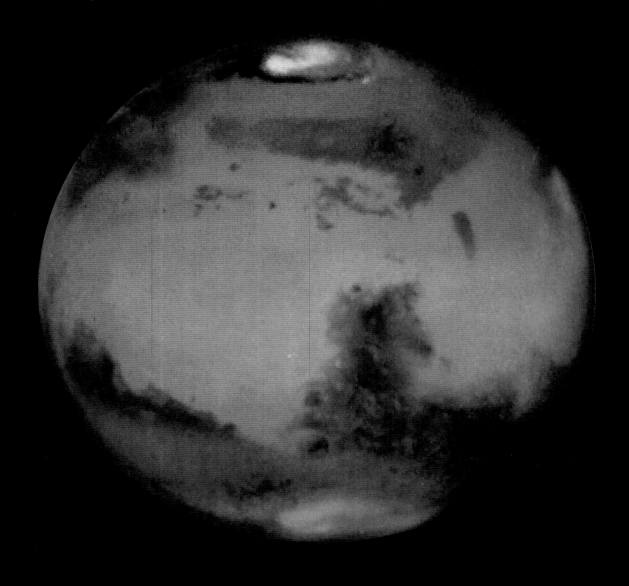

CHAPTER 3

What Is Mars Made Of?

The average surface temperature on Mars is −81°F!

Do you think Mars is more like Earth than most other planets? If you answered yes, you are correct in many ways. How is Mars like Earth?

The average surface temperature on Earth is about 59 degrees Fahrenheit (15 degrees Celsius). The coldest areas on both Mars and Earth are those that are farthest north and south.

The Surface of Mars

Mars is like Earth in many ways. Mars is a terrestrial (tuh-RES-tree-uhl) planet. A terrestrial planet is made mostly of rock. It has a solid surface. Earth, Mercury, and Venus are the other terrestrial planets in our solar system. As on Earth, people could stand, run, and jump on the hard surface of Mars.

Like Earth, Mars has volcanoes. The largest volcano on Mars is called Olympus Mons.

These two hills (background) were discovered in 1997. They are known as Twin Peaks. They are about 100 feet (30 meters) tall.

Olympus Mons is the highest volcano in the solar system.

Olympus Mons is roughly the size of the state of Arizona.

Olympus Mons is about 15 miles (24 km) high. That is three times higher than Mount Everest—the highest mountain on Earth!

Also like Earth, Mars has holes called craters. These craters were caused by asteroids, comets, and **meteorites** that crashed into the planets. Most of Earth's craters have been worn away by movements of water, wind, and land. Craters on Mars are not worn away as much. Mars still has thousands of craters. The biggest crater could hold the whole state of Texas!

Mars's winds can create giant sand dunes.

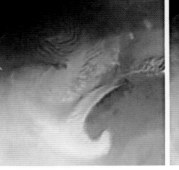

These photos show how vast Martian sand dunes changed during a storm.

Cold and Dusty

If you traveled to Mars, you would be traveling away from the sun. The farther you got from the sun, the less of its heat you would feel. So if you ever go to Mars, get ready to visit a very cold place.

The temperature of a planet depends on more than its distance from the sun. It also depends on its atmosphere. Earth's atmosphere traps a lot of the sun's heat. It holds the heat close to the planet. Mars has a thin atmosphere that doesn't trap much heat.

When you're not fighting the cold on Mars, you may be fighting giant dust storms. These reddish clouds of dust can last for weeks. Winds may blow up to 100 miles (161 km) per hour.

What's in the Air?

The atmosphere on Mars is very different from the atmosphere on Earth. On Earth, the atmosphere has plenty of oxygen. People need oxygen to breathe.

On Mars, the atmosphere is made mostly of a gas called carbon dioxide. There is some oxygen in the atmosphere. However, there is not enough oxygen for people to breathe.

A dust storm in 2001 covered nearly the entire planet (photo at right). It hid many of Mars's features.

The scientists were right. In 2006, another spacecraft took photos of the "face" from a different angle. Now it looked like a bunch of rocks. The face was an optical illusion. At certain times of day, the sun casts shadows that look like eyes, a nose, and a mouth.

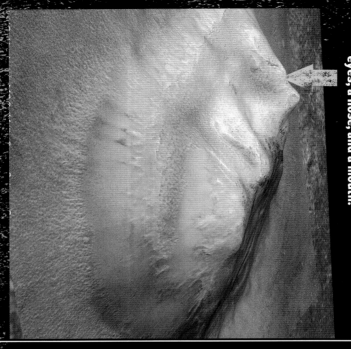

Galle

In 1999, the *Mars Global Surveyor* took another picture of Mars. It shows a crater called Galle that looks just like a happy face! It was created by natural features on the surface of Mars.

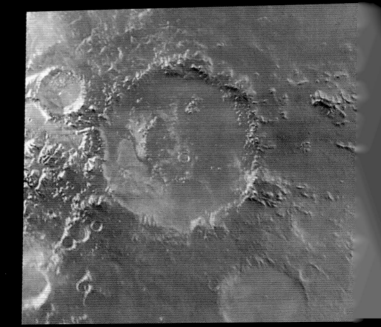

Put on a Happy Face

What do these Mars rock formations look like to you? Sometimes rocks and other natural formations can look like something else entirely!

Martian Face?

In 1976, the *Viking 1* space probe took many photos of Mars. One photo showed a rock formation that looked like a human face. Some people thought this was a sign of life on Mars, but scientists disagreed. They said that the face appeared because the sun's light hit the rock formation at a certain angle.

27

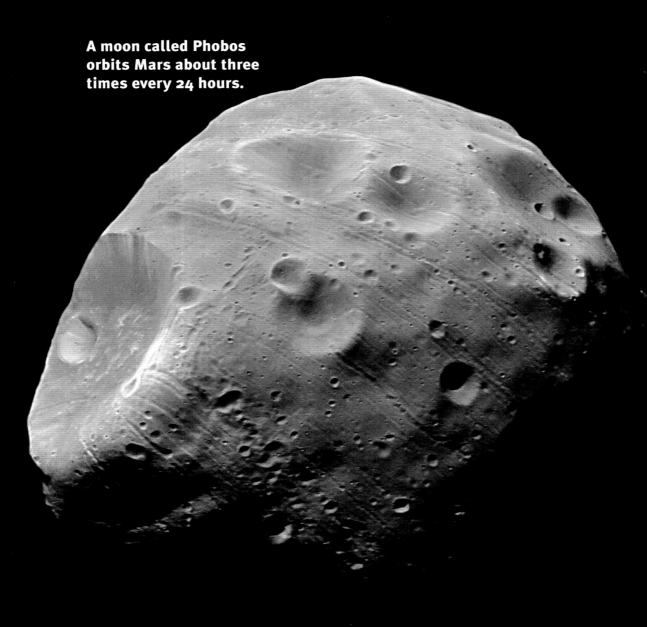

A moon called Phobos orbits Mars about three times every 24 hours.

CHAPTER 4

The Moons of Mars

Some scientists want to land on one of Mars's moons and study Mars from there.

When most people think of a moon, they think of the large, round moon that orbits Earth. However, Earth's moon is not a typical moon. Most moons in the solar system are much smaller. Many moons are not perfectly round, either. In fact, some have pretty strange shapes!

The light areas on the surface of Earth's moon are higher than the dark areas.

Earth has only one moon, but Mars has two. One of the moons is named Phobos (FOH-buhs), which means "fear." The other moon is named Deimos (DAY-mos), which means "panic." The moons were named by Asaph Hall, the American astronomer who discovered them in 1877. Mars is named after the ancient Roman god of war. Hall named the moons after the mythological sons of Mars.

Phobos and Deimos are both small and shaped like lumpy potatoes. Phobos is 14 miles (23 km) across at its widest point. It has a huge crater that covers nearly half of it. Deimos is only 7 miles (11 km) across. It is so small that 300 of these moons could be lined up across Earth's moon!

These two images of Deimos and Phobos have been placed side by side to compare their sizes. Deimos rises in the east and sets in the west. Phobos rises in the west and sets in the east.

Phobos

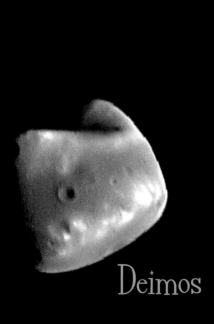

Deimos

Some astronomers think Phobos and Deimos might be asteroids that got trapped in their orbits around Mars. Gravity is slowly pulling Phobos closer to the planet. Astronomers say that this moon may crash into Mars in about 50 million years.

If Phobos crashes into Mars, its pieces could form a ring around the planet.

Phobos orbits only about 3,700 miles (6,000 km) above the surface of Mars. No moon in the solar system orbits closer to its planet.

Mars *Spirit*

Get a close look at *Spirit,* a robot that's helping astronomers study Mars. Turn the page and find out what astronomers are learning about the planet.

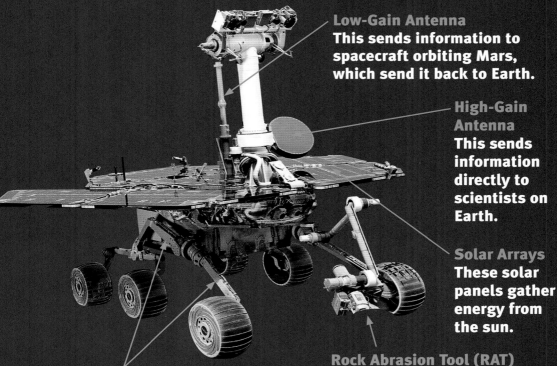

Low-Gain Antenna
This sends information to spacecraft orbiting Mars, which send it back to Earth.

High-Gain Antenna
This sends information directly to scientists on Earth.

Solar Arrays
These solar panels gather energy from the sun.

Rock Abrasion Tool (RAT)
This drill finds rocks and grinds them into dust. Other instruments next to the drill study the rocks and soil.

Rocker-Bogie Mobility System
These metal bars move up and down to keep all six wheels on the ground, so the vehicle won't tip over.

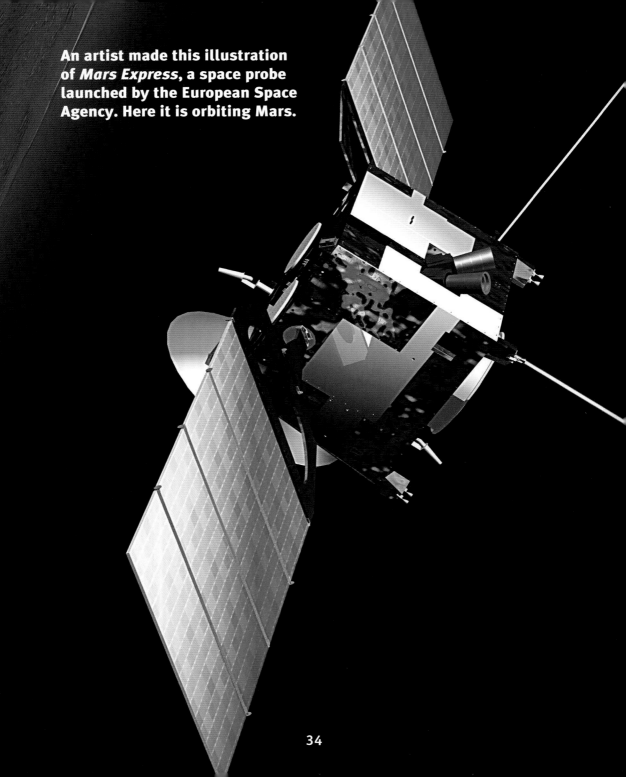

An artist made this illustration of *Mars Express*, a space probe launched by the European Space Agency. Here it is orbiting Mars.

CHAPTER 5

Missions to Mars

All life on Earth needs water to survive.

What do astronomers look for when seeking life on other planets? They study a planet's temperature, weather, and other conditions. Then they decide whether life might survive in such a place. One key ingredient they always look for is water.

Oceans cover nearly 70 percent of Earth's surface.

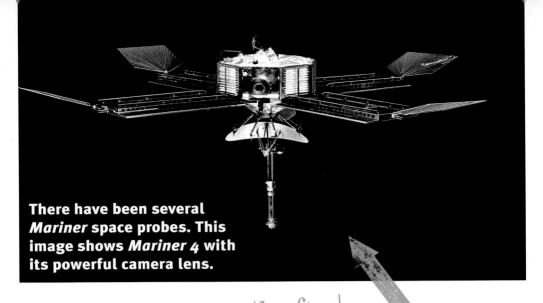

There have been several *Mariner* space probes. This image shows *Mariner 4* with its powerful camera lens.

Mariner 4 was the first spacecraft to photograph and transmit close-up photos of Mars.

Water on another planet is a sign that life might exist there. Would astronomers find water on Mars?

To get a good look at Mars, astronomers at the National Aeronautics and Space Administration (NASA) send up space probes. Space probes are spaceships that travel without astronauts in them. The first probes to get close to Mars were the *Mariner* probes.

The Mariner Missions

Four *Mariner* probes photographed Mars between 1965 and 1971. They sent back the first clear pictures of Mars. The pictures showed an empty, dry landscape. Astronomers got a good look at some craters and volcanoes, but they couldn't see any life or flowing water.

There was one exciting discovery, however. Pictures showed what looked like empty riverbeds. It seemed as though flowing water had once helped to form Mars's surface. Perhaps there had once been life on Mars as well.

Space probes are controlled by computers on Earth.

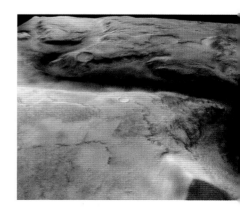

Mars Express took this image of the Reull Vallis. Scientists believe this river channel was once formed by flowing water on Mars.

The Viking Mission

Two *Viking* space probes flew to Mars in 1976. These probes carried **landers**. Landers parachute down from space probes and gather samples for further study.

The *Viking* landers tested rock and soil samples so astronomers could find out what Mars is made of. Astronomers could tell what gases are in the planet's atmosphere. They also looked for signs of life, but they did not find any.

Mars Exploration Timeline

1781–1784
British astronomer William Herschel makes maps of Mars. The maps feature lakes and rivers that he believed Martians enjoyed.

1965
The *Mariner 4* spacecraft flies by Mars and finds no sign of life.

The Mars Pathfinder Mission

The *Mars Pathfinder* spacecraft took along a small robotic **rover,** a type of vehicle that would explore Mars. *Pathfinder* bounced down onto the surface of Mars on July 4, 1997. Panels opened, and the six-wheeled robot called *Sojourner* rolled out onto the planet's surface.

1976
Viking 1 **(below) and** *Viking 2* **are the first spacecraft to land on Mars. They find places where life may have existed long ago.**

2002
The *Odyssey* **spacecraft discovers water ice below the surface of Mars. Is there life down there? Nobody knows.**

A NASA engineer poses next to *Sojourner* (left) and another rover, *Marie Curie* (right).

NASA scientists controlled *Sojourner's* movements from Earth. *Sojourner* explored the planet for more than a month. It sent thousands of pictures and test results back to Earth. Astronomers learned a lot more about the weather, soil, rocks, and atmosphere on Mars.

Sojourner's pictures showed rocks in strange formations. Astronomers think that great floods once pushed some Mars rocks together. This was another sign that Mars may have been a wet planet millions of years ago.

Many More Missions

More clues about life on Mars have been revealed. In 2000, the *Mars Global Surveyor* found more evidence that water may have flowed on Mars.

Astronomers have known that there was frozen water on Mars's south pole. A 2007 mission found more than expected. It found that the water ice is more than 2 miles (3 km) thick. It lies under a layer of carbon dioxide ice.

Mars's water ice layer covers an area larger than Texas!

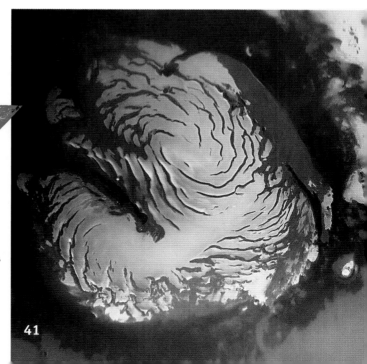

The Mars Global Surveyor took this photo of Mars's north pole. Light areas are believed to be left over water ice.

Rovers called *Spirit* and *Opportunity* rolled over large areas of Mars beginning in 2004. They tested rock and soil samples and took thousands of pictures. As of 2007, the rovers were still sending information to Earth from Mars!

Astronomers are planning more missions to Mars. Other people hope to send humans to Mars someday. Maybe in your lifetime, humans will go there. Who knows? You could be one of the first people to visit. ★

Mars rovers can travel up to 110 yards per day.

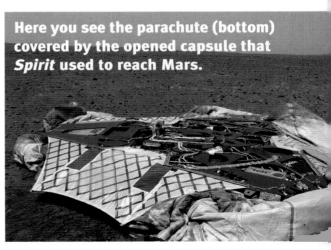

Here you see the parachute (bottom) covered by the opened capsule that *Spirit* used to reach Mars.

True Statistics

Discovered: Unknown

Classification: Terrestrial

Number of moons: 2, Phobos and Deimos

Atmosphere: Yes

Average surface temperature: −81°F (−62°C)

Average distance from the sun: About 142 million mi. (228 million km)

Length of a day: 24 hours, 37 minutes

Length of a year: 687 Earth days

A 100-pound (45 kg) person would weigh: 38 lb. (17 kg)

First lander: *Viking* on July 20, 1976

Age: About 4.5 billion years

Did you find the truth?

(F) You would weigh more on Mars than you do on Earth.

(T) There is a crater on Mars that looks like a happy face.

Resources

Books

Buckley, James. *Space Heroes: Amazing Astronauts*. New York: DK Books, 2004.

Chrismer, Melanie. *Mars*. Danbury, CT: Children's Press, 2008.

Deady, Kathleen W. *Space Walks*. Mankato, MN: Bridgestone Books, 2003.

Jackson, Ellen. *The Worlds around Us: A Space Voyage*. Minneapolis: Millbrook, 2006.

Shearer, Deborah A. *Space Suits*. Mankato, MN: Bridgestone Books, 2002.

Somervill, Barbara A. *The History of Space Travel*. Chanhassen, MN: The Child's World, 2004.

Tocci, Salvatore. *NASA*. Danbury, CT: Franklin Watts, 2003.

Vogt, Gregory. *Comets*. Mankato, MN: Bridgestone Books, 2002.

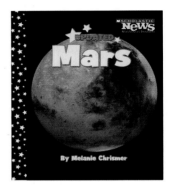

Organizations and Web Sites

NASA's Mars Exploration Program

marsprogram.jpl.nasa.gov/index.html
Check out this Web site for information on all of NASA's
Mars missions.

National Space Society

1620 I Street NW, Suite 615
Washington, DC 20006
202-429-1600
This organization works toward humans successfully living
and working in space.

Welcome to Mars!

marsprogram.jpl.nasa.gov/funzone_flash.html
Visit this Web site for fun games and activities about Mars.

Places to Visit

Kennedy Space Center

Kennedy Space Center,
FL 32899
www.ksc.nasa.gov
Explore NASA's launch
headquarters and learn
more about some of the
organization's space missions.

Smithsonian National Air and Space Museum

Independence Avenue at
4th Street, SW
Washington, DC 20560
202-633-1000
www.nasm.si.edu

Important Words

asteroids (AS-tuh-roidz) – large pieces of rock that orbit the sun

astronomers (uh-STRAW-nuh-murz) – scientists who study the planets, stars, and space

atmosphere (AT-mu-sfihr) – the blanket of gases that surrounds a planet or other object

axis (AK-siss) – an imaginary line that runs through the center of a planet or other object

comets – large chunks of rock and ice that travel around the sun

gravity – a force that pulls two objects together; gravity pulls you down onto Earth

landers – space vehicles that are designed to land on other planets or moons

meteorites (MEE-tee-uh-RITES) – space objects that have crashed into a planet

orbits – travels around an object such as a sun or planet

rover – space vehicle that explores the surface of another planet or moon

solar system (SOH-lur SISS-tuhm) – a sun and all the objects that travel around it

Index

About the Author

Award-winning author Elaine Landau has a bachelor's degree from New York University and a master's degree in library and information science from Pratt Institute.

She has written more than 300 non-fiction books for children and young adults. Although Ms. Landau often writes on science topics, she especially likes writing about planets and space.

She lives in Miami, Florida, with her husband and son. The trio can often be spotted at the Miami Museum of Science and Space Transit Planetarium. You can visit Elaine Landau at her Web site: www.elainelandau.com.

PHOTOGRAPHS © 2008: Corbis Images: 13 (Bettmann), 10 (Roger Ressmeyer), 7, 23 (Roger Ressmeyer/NASA); ESA: 6, 37 (DLR/FU Berlin/G.Neukum), 4, 26 top (DLR/FU Berlin/MOC/G.Neukum), 34 (Medialab); Getty Images: back cover (StockTrek), 8 (World Perspectives); JupiterImages: 9 (Hemera Technologies), 3 (StockTrek); NASA: 28 (ESA/DLR/FU Berlin/G.Neukum), 40 (JPL), 42 (JPL/Cornell), 33 (JPL/Cornell/Maas Digital), 26 bottom, 41 (JPL/MSSS), 11, 20, 22, 24, 31 (JPL-Caltech), 12 (JPL-Caltech/Cornell/NMMNH), cover (JPL-Caltech/USGS/Cornell), 39 right (NSSDC), 25 (STScl/AURA), 36; Pat Rasch: 16,17,19; Photo Researchers, NY: 27 (NASA), 5 top, 14 (Detlev van Ravenswaay); Phototake/Michael Carroll: 32; Photri Inc./NASA: 39 left; Scholastic Library Publishing, Inc.: 44; The Art Archive/Picture Desk: 38 left (Royal Society/Eileen Tweedy); The Image Works: 5 bottom, 38 right (NASA/SSPL), 21 (Photri/Topham); TIPS Images: 35 (Bildagentur).